Experience the World of Shad Fishing

To Mabel and MORT

May we fish for Shad soon

Lenox Dick

23 May 96

Lenox Dick

Frank Amato

PORTLAND

Dedication

To my dear son Hugh
who should have been part of this.

Published in 1996 by Frank Amato Publications, Inc.
P.O. Box 82112, Portland, Oregon 97282
(503) 653-8108
ISBN: 1-57188-062-3
UPC: 0-66066-00254-9
Cover Drawing: Tony Amato
Left Cover Photo: Bob Singley • Right Cover Photo: John Shewey
Book Design: Charlie Clifford
Printed in Canada
1 3 5 7 9 10 8 6 4 2

Contents

Acknowledgments

Our knowledge is based on the learning and experiences of past generations. With the assistance of the librarians at the Multnomah County Library in Portland, Oregon, I reviewed most of the pertinent literature about shad fishing from 1950 to 1995. Although I have fished for shad in Oregon for approximately 40 years, from both river bank and boat, my stream wading has been limited. My old friend and colleague, Donald Wysham, MD, has given me a great deal of assistance in wading and stream techniques.

One of the most important resources is the various fish and game commissions of those states that have shad runs in their streams and rivers. They all replied to my inquiries promptly. Their information is usually updated yearly. They supplied information on how and where to fish. The U.S. Fish and Wildlife Service is also a source of facts as they apply to the nation as a whole.

John Shewey has written a chapter on stream fishing for shad in his book, *Northwest Fly Fishing—Trout Beyond*, that is a classic (Frank Amato Publications, 1994, Portland, Oregon). Finally, I would like to bring to the attention of the reader the marvelous book, *Shad Fishing*, by C. Boyd Pfeifer, (Crown Publishing, 1975, New York, NY), which is unfortunately out of print.

I would also like to thank Brian Ilie and Ed Iyman, professional guides, for sharing their boat shad-fishing expertise; Arden Browning and Kevin Johnson of Fishermen's Marine Supply for their patient help in teaching me to use a sonar fish finder; and Lowrance Electronics for the technical data they supplied about sonar fish finders.

History

Shad were an important source of food for the Indians on the East Coast of America for many thousands of years. With the arrival of the white European settlers, they became important as a gourmet food and sport.

Shad also played an important part in American history. During the terrible winter of 1776-77, the ragged, starving Continental Army was camped at Valley Forge, Pennsylvania. By spring the army was in dire straits. One of the enlisted men, an angler, explored the Schuylkill River and found a large shad run. He caught some shad and ran back to camp. The soldiers swarmed to the river with rod, net and pitchfork. They caught shad and so provided welcome protein for the starving. It might be pushing history a bit, but one could claim that shad won the Revolutionary War.

Shad were important at the beginning of the last 100 days of the Civil War. General Thomas Rosser was the right-hand man of the South's best cavalry general, Jeb Stewart. General Rosser, known to indulge in food and alcohol intemperately, came upon a shad run in the Nattoway River, not far from Appomattox, Virginia. General Rosser succumbed to his weakness for fine food. He borrowed a seine and waded into the cold water with an Afro-American servant and several aides. They caught a number of big shad. It so happened that it was time to rest the horses and men. He decided to have a shad bake and invited General Pickett and General Robert E. Lee's nephew, General Fitzhugh Lee, a senior cavalry general, to a hickory-smoked shad bake. Both generals accepted; the shad bake was a great success. It lasted two or three hours. The generals were not worried; they thought their sector was calm. The Union troops broke through while they were resting, eating and talking. The Confederates were unable to restore their lines. This was the beginning of the last 100 days of the Civil War which resulted in Lee's surrender at Appomattox.

In 1871, white shad (American shad) were introduced into the Sacramento River system by order of Spencer Fullerton Baird, then head of the Smithsonian Institute. Baird sent Seth Green with Hudson River shad fry, by railroad, to this river system. Shad were introduced into the Columbia River system approximately in 1890. These two introductions of shad fry resulted in large shad runs in many of the rivers of the West Coast, extending from Mexico to Alaska.

On the East Coast during the usual three months of shad fishing, shad meat and shad roe are expensive items on the menus of fine restaurants.

Many gourmets feel this is the finest tasting of all fish. On the West Coast, despite the large shad runs in California, Oregon and Washington, people seldom eat anything but the roe and throw the shad away. Shad caught by an angler is the cheapest fish to catch and eat; unfortunately the numerous bones and lack of knowledge of boning has prevented their becoming as desirable a table fish as they are on the East Coast. (At the back of this book is a description and photographs on how to bone a shad.)

Over the years, shad fishing has become increasingly popular. Some shad runs on Pacific Coast rivers have become the largest of any anadromous (ocean-returning) fish. Some shad runs on the East Coast are in dire straits.

Biology

All shad lay their eggs by broadcasting them on the surface of the water. Temperature has a great deal to do with spawning. When the female extrudes between 50,000 to 500,000 eggs, or roe, it is a frantic turbulent process that takes place at night. The male swims alongside the female, frequently bumping into her as she lays her eggs. The bumping is seen by some as an aid to laying the eggs. The eggs then sink to the bottom and hatch in about six days. The fry lose their yolk sacs in about a month. They remain in the stream or river all summer until they reach five to six inches in length in the fall. At this time, they swim out into the ocean. They make a marvelous source of food for predator fish such as squawfish and walleyes.

White shad spawn in the main parts of streams or rivers. Hickory shad spawn in tributaries of rivers or large streams. White shad will not bite at night. Hickory shad will bite while spawning in the dark, and anglers take advantage of this. Hickory shad are considered even better fish for catching on a fly than white shad, and their roe even more of a delicacy than that of white shad. They are found in the South.

One hundred years after shad were introduced into West Coast streams, genetic studies show that there is such a genetic difference between West Coast and East Coast shad, that it may not be wise to bring West Coast shad eggs to the East Coast to help restore diminished shad runs, although this was done in the 1960s.

Shad are plankton eaters in the ocean. They, like other anadromous fish such as salmon, do not feed during their spawning run; yet, they will take bait such as worms, minnows, flies and lures of all types. At the present time I can find no theories as to why plankton eaters attack lures, flies and bait. Some experts feel this is an anger reflex.

White shad are usually four to five years old at the time of their first spawning run. Their average weight is three to five pounds. The males are usually much smaller than the females. Big males are often the size of small females. Here is a method for telling the difference: Apply gentle pressure on the abdomen by running thumb and index finger gently down to the vent. White milky fluid indicates a male; reddish indicates a female.

About 30 percent of shad are repeat spawners. Some shad live to be eight or nine years of age. Shad from southern regions where streams and rivers become exceptionally warm in summer do not have repeat spawners in their spawning runs.

After hatching, high water flood conditions can deplete the population of the year's young. The Hudson and Delaware rivers had their runs blocked for many years by pollution barriers at Philadelphia and New York City. With the successful decrease in pollution, shad runs are gradually returning to many of the previously afflicted East Coast rivers. On the West Coast the runs in most of the rivers have continued to increase. The largest fish run in Oregon and Washington's Columbia River system is shad. This run averages about three million.

West Coast anglers have no problem as far as recognition of shad. There are only white shad.

On the East Coast the differences in appearance between white and hickory shad are as follows: A white shad's lower lip is entirely enclosed in the upper jaw. Hickory shad have an easily visible projecting lower jaw.

On the East Coast, shad roe are considered a delicacy. In Charleston, South Carolina, fish markets in 1994 boned shad was selling for about $6 a fish. Shad roe is also very expensive when purchased on the East Coast.

Equipment

Spinning and Casting Rods and Reels

Just about any spinning rod can be used to catch shad. Fishing just below Bonneville Dam when the shad are running well is a shoulder-to-shoulder proposition in the favorite areas. You will see just about every type of spinning rod and reel. Most are five to seven feet in length and relatively limber. I have also seen typical surf casting outfits with long, heavy rods and big casting reels. Some anglers use typical eight or nine foot steelhead rods with casting reels. Most of these rods are high-modular graphite that will cast from three-eighths up to two ounces of lead.

Spinning rods with spinning reels should be capable of holding 100 yards of six to 12 pound test soft monofilament line. For bank fishing, I like a nine-foot rod rated for casting a one-sixteenth to three-eighths ounce lure. These modern high-modular graphite spinning rods, although labeled as suitable for one-sixteenth to three-eighths ounce weights, can easily cast one-ounce lures. It is most important that they can cast one-sixteenth ounce lures, because at rare times shad go into what has been described as a surface feeding frenzy. A better term for this is a biting frenzy.

I am also asked: "What about a typical bass outfit?" They can be used for trolling or on a boat that is anchored in current, but it takes a true expert to cast a one-sixteenth ounce lure any distance.

Spinning Reels

Cheap reels will work for a time; then their drags become unreliable and when a shad makes an initial run they will suddenly seize up, and good-bye shad. Good-bye fishing, unless you have spare cheap spinning reels.

Spinning reels also have the unfortunate habit of developing line snarls in the reel which are time-consuming to untangle. Often they require removal of about half of the line on the reel. I used to take off too little line and the blood knots, which I use to attach new line, would suddenly get involved with the guides, the cast would slow down and distances would be decreased. Hence, one-half the line, or 50 yards, should be removed and then new line reattached. The angler must remember that line on the spool should fill the spool to about one-sixteenth to one-eighth-of-an-inch below the lip of the spool for best casting.

It is also wise to have an extra spinning rod in your automobile. Rods break when casting extra heavy weights and when you are trying to release snagged lures.

Casting Rods and Multiple-Geared Bait and Lure Casting Reels

These rods and reels, of the type used in steelhead fishing, are ideal for boat fishing. True spinning reels can be used, but when a boat is anchored in fast water (1 1/2 to 3 miles per hour) the ability to thumb a casting reel and find bottom with a sinker is much easier than when using a spinning reel. This will be further explained in the chapter on boat fishing.

Lines for Spinning Reels

I find the big spools of inexpensive soft monofilament found in most shops do very well. Many anglers use six-pound monofilament. I have found six-pound to break too easily, and prefer eight-pound.

Lines for Casting Reels

Inexpensive soft nylon that comes on spools works well. For main line on the casting reel, eight or ten-pound test is sufficient. This line should be changed every year. It is apt to become stiff over time and not cast well.

Fly Fishing Equipment

Fly Rods

The best all-around fly rod for any type of fly fishing is a nine-foot graphite rod for either a five or six weight fly line. My own rod is for a five-weight line but I use a six weight line to load the rod for better casting.

Fly Reels

You need a fly reel that holds 100 yards of backing, is priced in the $30 to $60 range and has a good drag and rim control spool that can be easily palmed.

Fly Lines

A fly line is as important as a fly rod. You may need various lines: floating line, a moderate-weight sinking line and finally a high density sinking line.

Forward taper fly lines are best suited for shad fishing because they cast farther. Now the selection becomes tough. Looking through a large mail order fishing catalog, I found the following choices:

• Regular weight floating fly line.

• Floating fly line with front 10-foot sink tip that sinks 1 1/4 to 2 inches per second.

• Floating line with 10-foot sink tip that sinks 3 1/2 to 5 1/2 inches per second.

Shooting Head Fly Lines

The shooting head is 30 feet. They can be purchased with loops on both ends that can be quickly changed on the running line. In the above-mentioned catalog there are five heads, the last is a lead-core shooting head which sinks even faster than five inches a second, and is more difficult to cast and control.

Instant Sink-Tip System

You can use your regular floating line and add six feet of sinking line. They also come in four sinking rates, the same as previously described lines. These lines are more difficult to cast and create a definite splash when landing in the water, but they get the fly down to the fish.

After much discussion with many of my shad-fishing and trout-fishing friends, the consensus is they like the shooting head best and the sink-tip next.

Emergency Sink-Tip Fly Line

If you have forgotten your sink-tip fly line or shooting head fly line, twist-on lead is one product that can help you out of this jam. Take three strips of twist-on lead. Twist on one strip just above your leader knot, then two more strips 12 inches apart. A short leader of three or four feet with one or two twist-ons, spaced apart on the leader, will increase the sink rate. This is no substitute for a commercial line; it splashes on landing and has a tendency to hinge. I have been successful in using it when I have forgotten my sinking line, or when my sinking line fails to reach the desired depth.

Other Equipment

Most bank casters keep their lures in a tackle box. I believe that tackle boxes belong in the automobile. They are a nuisance to carry from place to place, hence, I use a canvas bag with a strap that goes over my shoulder. Lures, flies and other equipment are kept in small five-inch by four-inch clear, divided plastic boxes, along with an extra spinning reel.

When shad fishing streams, I use the same vest I use for trout and salmon fishing, which has a built-in life preserver. Depending on the stream temperature, I use regular neoprene waders.

Other important items: a collapsible jackknife that contains scissors, a little gadget to remove varnish from the eyes of flies and lures and a pair of needle-nose pliers with the ability to punch small holes in pencil-leads. I use a fish stringer to keep shad alive by keeping them in the water. A fish stringer has a heavy needle on one end, I pierce the upper and lower lips, thus keeping the mouth shut and allowing water to circulate through the fish's gills.

Landing Nets

Where I fish a conventional wood-handled trout-landing net, grafted to a five-foot pole is the best net for bank shad fishing. The reason for a long-handled net is that the large rocky banks on the Columbia River extend out into the river, and it is usually impossible to beach fish. Consequently, the long handle allows the angler, or a fellow-angler, to reach out and net the fish. Occasionally a spot will be found where a shad can be beached.

Anglers under the age of 40 can leap about these rocks with abandon. A long-handled landing net also makes an excellent staff for elderly anglers to keep their balance on the Columbia River below Bonneville Dam. The rocks are so large I spend a lot of time crawling over them. The Columbia River bank is a leg-breaker.

For wading streams, typical short-handled trout nets are also used. The shad is not an easy fish to land by hand. They are very active and much harder to hang onto than other freshwater fish.

Flies, Darts, Lures & How to Make Them

hen a steelhead is ready to take an attractor fly, lure or bait it will take almost anything as long as it is the proper size. Not so, the shad. Of all the various game fish I have attempted to catch, shad are the most finicky. Year in and year out, shad seem to prefer darts. One expert shad fisherman wrote that he has 400 shad darts in his kit. They vary in size, with numerous colors and shades, but most are in small sizes. When in doubt, go to a smaller size. In early spring with cloudy water, quarter ounce darts are fished deep. As the water clears and lowers, the knowing shad fisherman reduces the dart size to three-sixteenths ounce, one-eighth ounce, one-sixteenth ounce or even one thirty-second ounce.

In the past 10-plus years, most darts have been painted with fluorescent paint; most hooks are plain wire, gold or silver. Recently, a chartreuse head with green body and no tail has become popular. Small things such as the proper hook and color make a difference. Shad are unpredictable and change their preference in a matter of hours or even minutes. Consequently, the wise angler carries various intensities of color combinations. Color combinations include: red head/yellow body; all black; all hot orange. Other colors in various shades work as well: green, black, pink and purple, as well as black head/pink body, black head/purple body, black head/orange body, red and chartreuse. The combinations of colors are infinite.

When fishing from the bank, as well as from a boat, I have seen shad ignore all darts, flies, color combinations, spinners, spoons and take only plain gold hooks, plain bronzed hooks, or plain silver hooks, or all of the above with three or four various colored beads attached on the leader above the hook. I've also seen them take a gold or plain hook with a few strands of various colored Flashabou. In recent years when fished from an anchored boat, tiny spinners, spoons (wobblers), some gold or silver, seem to work better than darts. Spoons that are silver or gold on one side and a color combination on the other also work well. One of the best lures in 1995 was a brass swivel with a plain hook attached.

Just think of the expense for the man who has 400 different darts! A package of two darts in 1995 cost $.89. This adds up to $178—Wow! That's a lot of money. Not that I think you must have that many darts, but you do need a lot. Most commercial darts come only in about 3 or 4 colors. Hence if you want more colors you must make your own or buy them without any paint on them. What is the answer? Make your own. Just like the dedicated trout fisherman makes his own flies. A simple trout fly costs $1.75 today and like darts, spinners and spoons, the loss rate can be extreme. At the end of the chapter, I will show you how to make your own shad lures, spinners and flies. Spoons are very difficult to make.

I have noticed recently that many anglers have changed to round lead-headed jigs (crappie jigs). They come with feathered tails like the tails on darts, which most fishermen cut off. They come in three sizes with about every color combination you can think of and cost about 15 cents each, or you can tie your own for 8 cents each. They are very simple to tie. These can be bought at many sporting goods stores that sell bass, crappie, walleye and salmon equipment. Stores such as K-Mart and Wal-Mart often sell such equipment.

Similar stores are found in towns on the East Coast. If not, there are catalog stores such as Cabella's, 1812 - 13th Avenue, Sidney, Nebraska, 69160, and Jann's Sports and Supplies, 3350 Briarfield Blvd., Maumee, OH 43537.

Making Your Own Darts and Spinners

Both Cabella's and Jann's Sports mail order stores sell all the supplies you need. I make shad darts and spinners; I do not make any other lures.

This photo shows a dart lead mold with darts in the mold. Beside the mold is an unpainted one and also darts which have been finished. All the casting can be done on your kitchen stove. It is essential that, besides the mold, you have a pouring ladle. Any aluminum pot will serve to melt the lead. Aluminum melts at a much higher temperature. The mold, hooks, 2-oz. ladle and lead at 1995 prices will cost about $30. You also need a base white paint, such as Rustoleum, and various colors of fluorescent paint. The amount of money this represents equals about 200 painted darts.

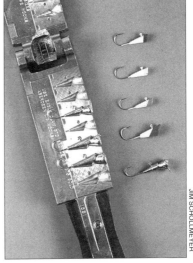

Small Spinners and Beads

I do not use stainless steel wire to make these. I use 10 or 12 pound

Mold for making lead jigs.

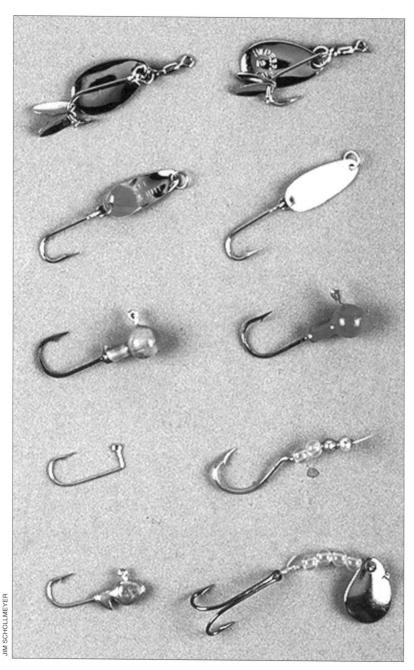

JIM SCHOLLMEYER

Various types of shad gear including spinners, spoons, beads and jigs.

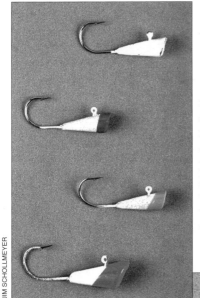

The shad dart is an old favorite available in many color combinations.

monofilament on which I tie a hook, single or treble. Then I attach the spinner blade with a clevis. Spinner blades can be purchased in various colors or you can paint your own. You can now purchase clevis that allow various colored blades to be changed at will. By doing this you will have a spinner for about one-tenth the commercial cost.

Flies

Shad flies and lures are interchangeable. A fly rod can fish a dart, small spinner, spoon, etc., just as well as a spinning rod. At times, shad flies seem best and can be fished in place of darts and lures. No stores to my knowledge sell shad flies. Many standard flies from size 12 to size 4, if sparsely tied, can be used for shad.

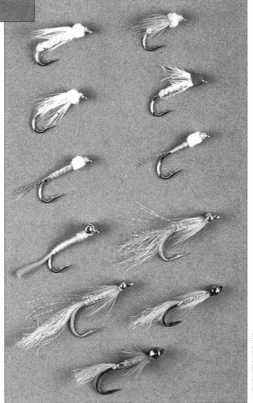

Shad flies are colorful and usually feature reds, whites, greens and yellows.

Fishing for Shad on the Main Umpqua River
Donald Wysham

t had rained heavily the preceding day when we arrived at the boat ramp on the main Umpqua River, near Umpqua Store, where the three of us were somewhat dismayed to see a cloud of muddy water flowing into the river from Calapooya Creek which entered the river just above the boat ramp. Gary Lewis' clients (our guide) had caught about 30 shad on weighted crappie jigs that morning but he felt the water might be too cloudy for fly fishing.

We therefore headed downstream about two miles to a well-known spot where the water was clearer; well known as a good fly fishing drift for shad. At this point there is a set of rapids which enter a large pool. On the south bank, there are steep ledges along which shad tend to congregate where they are successfully caught by spin fishermen with weighted jigs. However, according to Gary Lewis, the school of shad tends to circle around the pool and periodically will swim by the north bank which has a sloping rock bottom. It is possible to wade out to within casting distance of the seam where the main stream enters the pool. The shad congregate on the inside of the seam toward shore.

Gary has fished for shad since he was a boy. He points out that by far the most useful fly color is lime green (or chartreuse) and flies should be sparse. To emphasize this he points out that as a boy he and his friends would put a single scale on a hook then they would throw shad scales into the water and this was sufficient to attract shad. Gary recommends a type three full sinking line. He was using about 30 feet of sinking line as a shooting head backed by Amnesia monofilament. With this he could cast more than halfway across the pool. I was using a type two sinking line which seemed to work about as well.

The technique is to cast about 35 to 45 degrees upstream and allow the line to swing around so it is about 45 degrees downstream, then pause and let the line sink for a few seconds, next start a retrieve of fairly slow strips about a foot each. The shad don't hit hard but there is no question when one has a bite. When they are hooked, they vary in their fighting ability. Some

are "hot" fighters, take out a lot of line and jump repeatedly like mini tarpon. Others put up a more stubborn and dogged fight using their flat side to markedly increase the resistance.

Fishing tends to be best in early morning and late evening, just before and after the sun hits, or leaves, the water. Fishing in the evening, despite the cloudy water conditions, with visibility at about only two feet, we were getting a strike on about every second or third cast. We were having sufficient action so we could get some idea of the difference between flies. Bob Petersen, the third member of our trio, was using a relatively large and bushy fly and had virtually no success. Gary was using one of his favorites, a small fly with a chartreuse head and small tail with a few fibers of Krystal Flash. He had consistent success with this fly but I seemed to have more success with a modified bonefish fly. I tied this fly several years ago from a pattern based on a shrimp imitation, but with colors more suitable for shad. I call it the Shad Shrimp Fly. Gary switched to this fly and his success rate improved. Meanwhile, I had landed about 15 shad between one and one half and three and a half pounds, probably all males. (The females tend to be larger and come up the river later).

We finally persuaded Bob Petersen to switch to the Shrimp Fly and on his first and second casts he was into shad. By this time the sun had long since gone beyond the hill and it was getting dark; but Bob couldn't be persuaded to stop fishing and had to be dragged reluctantly from the shad holes so we could move downriver to the take-out point.

It may be worth noting that we did not use weighted flies and the flies did not have the metal-bead eyes that have been recommended in the past for shad flies. The pattern for the Shad Shrimp Fly is as follows: hook: size 8 or 6; materials: fluorescent lime green tying thread, lime green chenille, Teeny insect green feather and lime green Krystal Flash.

After we had fished for awhile and caught a number of shad we sat down on the bank. I asked Gary what makes a good site for shad fishing.

Gary replied: "This pool and rapid has been a hot spot for years. If you look carefully, you will see that in the rapids there are several slots. Shad like slots. The water that goes through must be fast but there probably is a critical speed of flow that shad like. You will notice that the pool is about 75 feet in diameter and I have already described the currents and its direction. We did well with our flies on our side of the pool and the spin fishermen did equally well fishing with weighted jigs in the slots on the other side. So to sum it up, shad like relatively shallow pools, current and slots running into it with fast water."

"Okay, Gary. We passed several places that looked like that and you kept on going."

"Don, there are numerous areas that look good but never have been. Frankly, nobody seems to know why. I know where the good areas are from experience. Incidentally, one of things we could have done with our fly is to twitch it on the retrieve."

"Well and good. What would you advise someone who does not know where to fish and comes to this river?"

"Easy—go where the crowd is. The problem with that is on weekends sometimes it is impossible to get to the popular spots because of the crowds. Fortunately, the crowd does not know all our secret spots. If you have a friend who wants to fish the Umpqua or other coast streams but does not want a guide, tell him to come on Saturday and Sunday but not to fish. Simply go up and down the river and see where the fly fishermen are fishing and how the catch is. Then on Monday, when there are very few people, go to those areas that you know are good. There will be just as many shad there as the day before. Later, after he has caught a lot of shad, he should explore the stream. He may find some of our secret spots."

In the course of reviewing the literature on shad fishing, one of the authors described this incident: He was carefully fishing a riffle that emptied into a pool. He was having good fishing when an elderly angler walked right in front of him. The writer complained with lots of expletives deleted.

The old man turned to him and said, "Relax; it won't disturb your fishing. Shad are so intent on going upstream it does not bother them."

The writer, much to his amazement, found this to be true. He kept on catching shad after the old man departed.

When fishing small and medium-sized streams that have a good flow, the principles described above hold for both white and hickory shad. One difference is that hickory shad, when spawning in a pool, can be caught at night.

Bank Fishing

e are going bank fishing, with both spinning rod and fly rod. We will fish just below Bonneville Dam. It is early in the season and the water is high. We will fish with either of these rods, a nine-foot graphite spinning rod with an eight-pound monofilament line, and a nine-foot graphite fly rod with a size 6, #3, 30-foot shooting head line and an eight-pound, six-foot tapered leader. Shad are generally on the bottom or close to it. Only rarely are they found in the upper one-third of the water column. We must be able to adjust both spinning and fly line to any depth. With the spinning rod we can add or subtract weight. With a fly rod we can sink the tip to the bottom or just under the surface by the speed with which we strip line.

We arrive at the dam and are as close to the spillway as is allowed. The bank here is very steep with immense riprap boulders. It is about 100 yards to the river. The Corps of Engineers built an easy trail down to the river; a sop to the masses. I hate the Corps, in every sense of the word, for what they have done to the ecology of the Northwest. Enough of that, let's go on with our fishing.

We are standing at the top of the bank. Let's stop and observe the river. It is Saturday and the bank is lined with anglers for about 200 yards. Interestingly there are very few native-born Americans. Most are Ukrainians, Russians, Poles, Japanese, Vietnamese, Hmong and others. You will hear very little English spoken here; these people are fishing for food

Shad fishing below Bonneville Dam on the Washington side.

and so am I. I love boned shad and fried shad roe.

Now, let's look at the river again. You will notice a definite current next to the shore. This is good. In the latter part of the season, the Corps of Engineers dropped the river level which caused the attractor currents to move out to the middle of the river, and so did the shad. The same thing goes on in the East. The shad stack up below the dams. It is likened to a crowd waiting for an elevator. Now watch, soon we will see a certain place in the line where more shad are being caught. That's where we are going.

We will not use our fly rods here because we would catch more anglers than shad. About one-half-mile down the river there are no fishermen fishing from the bank. There is room for a high back cast. To me it is strange that so many of these anglers don't explore downriver. Thank goodness they don't. I called up a friend who was here yesterday. He told me that the hot lure is a plain brass swivel with silver hook. Let us now rig up. There are two popular methods for rigging our spinning rods: hollow pencil lead in the line above the leader and a swivel; or a swivel with a pencil lead attached to the snap and then a leader of two and a half feet with a lure attached to the end.

On our fly rod we attach a Wysham Shrimp to a three-foot leader. We will not use it here. Later we will use this fly when we go down to the area where there are no shad fishermen.

With anglers alongside you, you have to time your casting to your neighbor's. Cast about 10 degrees upstream. Keep a tight line. Sometimes

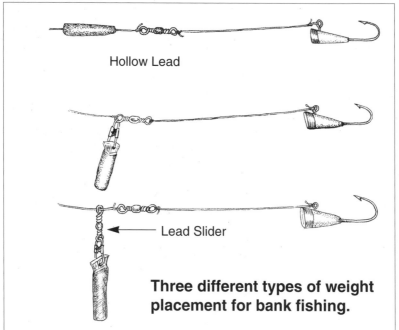

Hollow Lead

Lead Slider

Three different types of weight placement for bank fishing.

DÜRTEN

you allow your line to drift down without reeling. Other times, when it is about 30 degrees below, you can start reeling slowly. Occasionally start reeling slowly just as soon as the lure hits the water. Vary your casting depth and retrieves

Many times I have been next to an angler who is catching shad on the same lure, same weight and same length line, when I am not. It is evident that there are other variables to consider. How thick is his line? If it is thicker or thinner than mine I will not get the same depth as he does. What is the length of his leader? It should be about two and a half feet long. Too short a leader is a common fault. What angle is he casting upstream? Is he reeling faster or slower? Where does he start to reel? How much weight is he using? The length of the cast is also very important.

An Oregon Department of Fish and Wildlife biologist told me shad like to swim upstream in single file. Then he laughed. Actually they probably migrate in columns of three to six feet wide. The columns seem to shift from side to side. This is most noticable in boat fishing. The boat next to you will be catching shad and you won't, and then suddenly it will shift to your boat.

We have been here an hour and a half, we have caught 12 shad between us. Nobody has caught any shad for half an hour. This is probably not because we need a lure change. We are most likely between waves of shad. Remember shad come in waves. It is not unusual that an hour may pass before the next wave arrives. Also, especially in the middle of a bright

Long-handled nets are handy on the Columbia below Bonneville Dam.

day, they may stop biting altogether and start again late in the afternoon or at dusk. Let's move down one-half-mile to the fly water. If we cannot get our fly out far enough, we can use the spinning rod.

We are now down to the fly water and nobody is here. The current is about 50 feet from shore. However, I have had good fishing even when I cannot see any distinct current with a seam. A seam is a distinct line between the fast and slow water. With a fly rod, cast upstream about 30 degrees; when it is parallel to you, put in an upstream mend. After that allow the line to straighten. You can vary this presentation by waiting until the line is parallel to you and then twitching the rod tip, or pulling the line about four inches at a time, next to the reel. Remember, most of the time shad are on the bottom so if you are not catching shad use a heavier sinking line and a weighted fly. If after you have been catching shad they stop biting for about 15 minutes it may be that a change of fly is needed, or the next wave has not appeared. A good fly fishing spot will be good for spinning but a good spinning spot may not be good for flies because of limited back cast room. This may be due to a high bank, too many people or too deep a stream.

Sonar Fish Finders

hen fishing on a lake or river I always have a sonar fish finder in my boat. What is a fish finder? It is a computerized device that projects high frequency sound waves (sonar) to the bottom of the lake or river by means of a trans-

Humminbird Wide Vision.

ducer. These waves bounce off objects and the transducer in turn picks up these waves and returns them to a computer which makes them into an image on a liquid crystal screen, somewhat like a television screen. It has two major modes, automatic and manual. On automatic the returning sound waves, when bounced off a fish, return to the computer which projects them on the screen as fish symbols. Unfortunately, these symbols are often made by eddy currents, debris and weeds which the computer cannot distinguish from a fish. In the manual mode the computer shows all of the signals that return to the screen and at a depth past 30 feet it will differentiate fish more accurately as arches. Above 20 feet there may be half arches or straight lines. There are other features on these machines which are shown as a screen menu.

Fish finders are particularly good when fishing for shad, walleye, sturgeon, salmon and trout and steelhead in large rivers and lakes. Most every boat angler who has a fish finder agrees their most important feature is the ability to determine depth, define underwater structure and softness or hardness of the bottom. By structure I mean horizontal ledges both in the middle of the river and ledges close to the bank, big sunken rocks, sunken stumps and logs, etc. They are especially valuable for the sturgeon fisherman who seeks the deep holes in the river where sturgeon love to hide.

Depending on the size of the fish and its location, salmon and trout are more readily seen than walleye and sturgeon which are bottom-hugging fish, hence difficult to see with a fish finder. Professional walleye, shad and sturgeon guides, and some amateurs, can see all of these bottom fish constantly in the manual mode.

A fish finder is as difficult to program as a VCR. Like a VCR once the ability to program in the manual mode is learned, the full potential of a fish finder will be realized.

In the manual mode most machines are able to show true fish in the form of arches, depth, bottom contour and zoom. Zoom features allow the operator to concentrate on various levels of the water column. The very expensive models have split screens. One screen shows the whole water column while the second screen can zoom in on a specific depth.

The more expensive machines show water temperature and speed of boat. The expensive models include GPS (Global Positioning System), which allows the angler to plot where he has gone on the water and to return to that exact location at a later date.

Fish finders have improved every year. Let us hope they can make them simpler in future years so that the amateur will find them easier to use.

Boats and Anchoring for Shad

*T*he Columbia is a very large, powerful river and is mighty dangerous. The closer you come to power dam tailout rapids, the more dangerous it becomes. There are many precautions one should take. For example, on the Columbia, from Bonneville Dam about six miles downstream, the safest boat is 18 to 20 feet long with a special anchoring system. A boat that ventures up to the legal boundary at Bonneville Dam cannot hold against the current with a conventional Danforth fluke anchor. The current runs in this tailwater rapid at 10 miles per hour or more.

Easy Marine Products (Box 722, Troutdale, Oregon 97060) developed a side-by-side double fluke anchor. The post collapses on the anchor making it easy to store. This anchor is attached to the anchor- retrieving system.

Since 1980, there have been at least 12 capsizings, 2 drownings and numerous close calls due to improper achoring in the hazardous current.
The river is over 100 feet deep in places. At least 7-10 times the depth is recommended for anchor line length. The use of an anchor float is also strongly advised.
Cooperatively placed by the US Army Corps of Engineers and the Oregon Water Safety Council

Sign along Columbia River near boat launch.

Boaters on any river should wear life preservers. It is amazing how many do not. No matter how expert the guide or angler who is running the boat, a fatal accident can happen in moments.

In May 1995, an anchor rope tangled in the propeller of a boat attempting to anchor. The boat immediately turned stern first and was pulled under and sank. Nobody drowned in this accident; they were all wearing life pre-

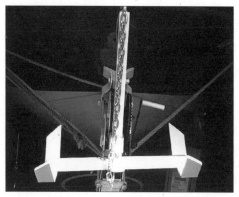

Big water anchor.

servers. Every skipper should have a sharp knife on his belt to cut the anchor rope in seconds.

Anchoring in any large river is a major undertaking demanding the proper equipment. Following are several anchor systems that are used below Bonneville Dam when fishing for shad, as well as in other parts of the river for sturgeon, where the current is strong and the depth is up to 100 feet.

Many boats now use either the Anchor Rite, Anchorlift or EZ Puller Locking Block. They all operate in the same general fashion: the large rocking-chair type anchor is dropped swiftly to the river bottom and much anchor line is released to reduce the angle of the anchor line to the buoy and boat. Depending on the current's flow you should use anywhere from seven to 10 times the length of the rope as the water is deep. Thus in moderate flowing water 30 feet deep,

Enjoying the day.

you might use about 200 feet of anchor line.

The anchor systems listed above feature very easy retrieval. When you want to move to another spot or return to shore you simply drive the boat upstream lifting the anchor to the buoy where it automatically locks. Then you simply gather in line and lift the anchor and attached buoy into your boat.

Anchor Rite   (503)-761-1059
AnchorLift   (503)-968-1330
EZ Puller Locking Block   (503)-492-4200

Anchor Safely (Army Corps of Engineers)
Swift currents, high flows and cold water make the following recommendations imperative

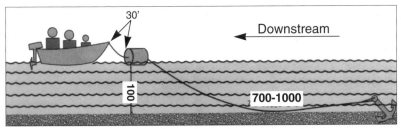

1. Use 7-10 times the depth of the water for the length of the anchor lines. River depth may exceed 100 feet in some places. Use a float for the anchor line (see the diagram) to serve as a buffer and reduce the risk of getting the anchor line tangled in the propeller.

Lower, do not throw, the anchor and avoid tangles in the line.

Anchor only off the point of the bow. Anchor off the stern or the side will capsize your boat.

2. Power upstream of anchor before retrieving it. Maintain position in the line with flow of current while retrieving anchor. Turning cross-wise to the current increases the risk of capsizing.

3. The Columbia River can become turbulent with little or no warning. You are advised to wear a Coast-Guard-approved floatation device at all times. Also, take precautions against hypothermia. River temperatures can range from the 70s in the summer to the 30s during the winter.

Boat Fishing

*T*oday is about the middle of June. Forty-six thousand shad went over Bonneville Dam yesterday. It is overcast with a slight drizzle. The Weather Bureau assures us that this will continue all day, so consequently we should have good shad fishing most of the day. Shad are apt to stop biting in bright sunlight, but not always. We launch my 16-foot 1973 Silver Liner with same-age Mercury 85 HP outboard. In the 1970s, this was used for water-skiing, but by 1985 all my children were married so I had the boat to myself. I have added a 7 HP Evinrude trolling and emergency motor, also of 1970s vintage. When I use

Willamette Falls at Oregon City during the flood of 1996. Each year hundreds of thousands of shad spawn below the falls.

this motor I have a special bar that attaches to the big motor and allows me to steer with the forward steering wheel.

We launch at the Beacon Rock ramp about four miles from the boat deadline below Bonneville Dam, then motor up about one and a half miles. We pass around a wide outward curve of land and on the upper part of the curve there are two boats anchored, while above the curve many more boats are anchored. The depth is 14 feet. The fish-finder shows a hard bottom which is undoubtedly gravel. Shad like hard gravel bottoms. Without the fish-finder we would not know the condition of the river bed. The current is 10 miles an hour. As we put out the anchor, a boat our size is drifting down the river. The skipper pulls up an ordinary fluke Danforth anchor and departs in obvious despair. There are boats all around us. Some are landing shad consistently. Two boats about 20 feet on each side of us are catching shad.

The fish-finder is on automatic mode. The upper part of the screen next to the surface is packed with fish symbols large and small. Just below the 10-foot mark on the screen, there are a few large fish symbols. We switch to the manual mode and the entire screen shows straight lines of various lengths and lots of turbulence and it is difficult to interpret. The fish-finder is switched again to the automatic mode and the screen clears. The top of the screen is again packed with small or medium fish symbols. These are probably the result of the marked turbulence and debris that makes the computer show symbols that are not fish. Between the 10-foot mark and the bottom the screen below 10 feet is clear. As we watch one or two large fish symbols appear. What is happening? These large fish symbols that appear on the part of the screen showing the bottom four feet of the water column are probably shad since they come and go. Most of the time shad swim close to the bottom. Considering that the cone width of the bottom we are seeing on the screen is about seven feet at this water level, these large fish symbols represent many shad.

The boats directly above and behind us are both catching shad. The boat to the left is not catching shad. This indicates to me that the shad column has moved over and is directly under us.

It is time to rig up. The most effective method is to rig with two lures, one above the other. With two rods out it is possible to use four different lures, giving the shad a greater choice. This is difficult to fish because of frequent tangles. Consequently, we will rig with single lures. Our casting line is 12-pound test monofilament and tied onto the swivel an 18" dropper line; to which is tied a two and a half foot eight-pound leader. To your leader, I will tie on a three ounce lead weight and a Dick-Knight spoon; to my leader I tie on a Triple Teaser spinner. In order to find the bottom we may have to change to a heavier lead.

Now the tricky part: Walking the lure back behind the boat. I like to have the lure about 30 to 50 feet behind the boat. I feel it is less disturbing to the shad. If the lead weight is too heavy, it will not bounce back along

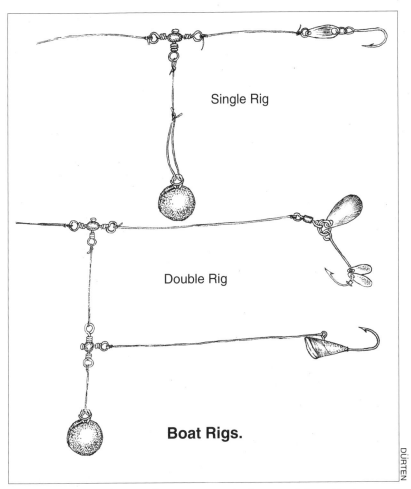

Single Rig

Double Rig

Boat Rigs.

DÜRTEN

the bottom; too light, it will not stay on the bottom. I drop the lure and lead overboard. Then I quickly raise the rod to vertical and at the same time allow the line to unreel under my thumb with a small amount of pressure on the spool. If there is not enough pressure, the line will go out too fast, and the thunk of the lead weight on the bottom will not be felt. If it is not felt, then two factors prevent this: the reel unwinds too fast or there is insufficient lead weight. Keep raising and lowering the rod so that you reach 30 to 50 feet distance behind the boat. At the end, raise and lower the rod several times. Each time you should feel the lure thunk on the bottom. Sometimes when you let out line, you have a very firm pull but never feel the bottom. This means the lead may be on the bottom, but the line is billowed out downstream. If the lead is on the bottom in this situation, you cannot feel the shad strike. If you are using two different lures on each line, you have a better chance of finding out the lure of the day. Of course, we could yell over to the next boat and find out what they are using.

Our lines are out and the rods are in the rod holders. We don't have to hold the rods because shad hook themselves.

There is one other method of fishing I have not mentioned: down-riggers. Down-riggers have their advocates. Salmon fishermen, both commercial and sport, use them in the ocean when fishing. A down-rigger consists of a large reel, usually with a metal cable attached. The cable passes over a short rod. The down-rigger is attached to the side of the boat. To the end of the cable is attached a heavy weight. Depending on the depth, a short leader with a clip on each end is clipped to the metal cable. The clip on the other end is attached to the line and lure. The advantage of this device is when a fish strikes, the lure is released and the fish can be played without any weight which, of course, makes playing the fish much more exciting.

No shad have taken our lure for half an hour and we have seen no fish symbols on the fish-finder screen. None of the boats around us have caught any either. This probably means we are between waves of shad. If the other boats are consistently catching shad, then we should move to a better location where we see fish symbols. However, if no boats are catching shad, then we are between waves of shad or the fishing may be over. The fishing will pick up usually later in the day about an hour before sunset.

Exploring for New Shad Fishing Locations

Shad stack up below dams, fish ladders, strong rapids and waterfalls. Examples of this are: Bonneville Dam on the Columbia River and Willamette Falls at Oregon City. The fish ladders on the Connecticut River are similar to the Columbia River. After looking at the rapids on the Potomac River near Washington DC, I think that just below them there must be good shad fishing. There are many other rivers on the East Coast with similar obstructions.

One thing to consider when looking for new shad areas is water level. An area with a good point of land or outward curve will be good in high water as long as there is a depth of 10 to 20 feet and current. By that I mean a place in the river with a sufficient current so that the water suddenly speeds up forming definite flow waves which are relatively narrow with a good seam. If, however, the water suddenly falls to the depth of only two or three feet with slow current there will be no shad.

We will anchor about 10 feet above this stone dock, and slightly to one side so our spoons and darts will be about 30 feet below the obvious narrow current. This should be a prime area. We will have our lures close to the bottom. After half an hour, no fish. The fish-finder shows medium-sized fish symbols near the surface, but none coming through close to the

Stone dock with two good seams.

bottom. What's wrong? My theory: The depth is 30 feet where our lures are. Behind the dock and next to the current is a back-eddy boil with a depth of 40 feet. I feel the water is too deep in the current, and shad dislike boils. Last year was a low-water year and a guide friend had consistently good fishing here. I did not ask him the water level, but I am quite sure it was much lower.

You ask: "All the shad must go by here to go on up to Bonneville Dam and on upriver. How and where do they go?"

I say this with reverence: "God only knows." I sometimes go up and down this river and find anglers with their boats anchored in places I would swear are poor locations to catch shad, but they are catching shad. One wise old owl once said to me, "Fish are where you find them."

Now we will go about one mile down-stream. I fished it four days ago; the water level was the same as it is today.

Point of land extending into river.

We anchor our boat about 200 feet above that point of land. What appears to be a point of land is actually the end of a 150-yard outward curve of the river. The river picks up speed about 50 yards before it reaches the point, thus producing a narrow riffle of about 15 feet in width with a seam. A seam is a distinct line between the fast and slow water. Our depth finder shows a hard 14-foot bottom, probably hard gravel or cobble (medium-sized stones close together). We are about 100 feet from shore and this is a classic shad location.

We have now walked our lures out about 50 feet, and the rods are in the rod-holders. I have mentioned this before. You do not have to hold the rod; shad hook themselves. The water is smooth here except in the riffle. There is an occasional large fish symbol showing on the screen of the depth-finder close to the bottom. There are no fish symbols in the upper part of the screen because of the lack of turbulence and debris. I feel the bottom fish symbols are shad. We will not see as many as below Bonneville Dam. They are only slowed down at this point and stacked up moderately, so we won't have fast and furious fishing. We have been averaging about one shad every 15 minutes. Today is late in the run so we are catching mostly large females which are the best to eat.

In the future when you are looking for shad look for them at the side of rocks, piers and at the end of jetties.

Shad Fishing in Southern Rivers

During the winter of 1994, I journeyed up the Atlantic Coast from Florida to South Carolina. Rivers and streams were slow and meandering and twisted around in numerous curves. There was a marked tidal flow that extended upriver for many miles.

In the middle of March I visited the St. Johns River in Florida. The run in this river comes in December. The river has such a slow current that fishing is almost all done by slow trolling with gasoline-powered outboards. No mention was made of use of quiet electric outboards. The same lures are used on the West and East coasts, and also in this river. I had the impression that very little bank fishing is done. This river does not have repeat spawning runs. The mature shad die after spawning because of high water temperatures which occur shortly after spawning. I just missed the shad runs, except in Georgia; unfortunately because of time I was unable to observe fishing by anglers.

The commercial season was on in Georgia, and I was able to watch boning of shad in Savannah. Here they can bone a shad in about five minutes. It takes my wife 15 minutes to do the same thing.

When I told them that shad on the West Coast were made into cat food and sturgeon bait, that only the roe was sold, and not much of that, they were incredulous. Boned, planked shad is a delicacy along the entire East Coast, as well as the roe.

Where to Fish for Shad

West Coast Shad Fishing

*F*ew shops that cater to fishermen have much information about shad runs. The state agencies that deal with this fish go under many different names. They are listed at the end of this chapter. I was impressed with the promptness with which they answered my queries, both by mail and phone. When I called the appropriate agency they would give me the names of the rivers that had runs of shad at that time, or if there was no current run. Then they would give the name and phone number of the biologist familiar with the particular rivers and streams. It takes some persistence to contact these individuals, but they can be reached and are most cooperative. They will tell you the best places to fish on the rivers and streams and at what time.

Shad runs on the West Coast are in excellent shape. The major rivers and smaller ones that go directly into the ocean are in good condition as far as shad are concerned.

The East Coast is a different story. There have been so many dams built since the 1800s that by 1950 the shad runs became almost extinct in rivers that once had magnificent runs. The history of the shad fishery and what is being done about it is best described by the U.S. Fish and Wildlife Service. I have taken the liberty of quoting from their shad bulletin:

"Today the Atlantic shad annual catch is at its lowest ever. Only about three million pounds were caught in 1984, down from 50 million pounds in the 1890s. The most precipitous decline along the Atlantic coast has occurred since 1970."

Shad in the Chesapeake Bay, Maryland

The Chesapeake Bay and Susquehanna River shad fishery became an important seasonal industry by 1870. From an annual harvest in the bay of 17.5 million pounds at the turn of the century, shad stocks fluctuated in an ever downward curve to landings around one million pounds today from the Virginia waters. After the harvest in the state fell to 25,000 pounds per year, Maryland placed a complete moratorium on the sport and commercial harvest after 1980. In Chesapeake Bay, shad once spawned in all major rivers. Migrations began in February and March and continued through May. In the old days on many of these rivers shad boats were so numerous one could cross the river by stepping from boat to boat.

The Susquehanna River, the Chesapeake's largest tributary, was once the bay's most important river for spawning shad. However, the Pennsylvania Canal system, built in the 1830s, required feeder dams at numerous locations that restricted migration to the lower 45 miles of the river. Later, four hydroelectric dams blocked migration still further.

On the East Coast the American shad has gone the way of the once prevalent Atlantic sturgeon. The striped bass seems to be heading in the same direction. Shad and sturgeon have two things in common: They spawn in bay rivers; and before they declined they were highly sought after for the superior quality of their flesh and eggs. Hope for anadromous and estuarine fish in Chesapeake Bay and other East Coast rivers lies in reversing the degraded water quality and habitat alterations that have created such problems.

Restoring the Shad

Shad restoration is underway or planned in 15 river basins from Maine to Virginia. The goal is self-sustaining runs of seven to nine million fish and reopening hundreds of miles of spawning habitat. The U.S. Fish and Wildlife Service supports these efforts by providing full-time biologists to coordinate restoration and management programs undertaken by state and federal cooperators. The service provides direct engineering and research assistance and financial support through federal and state cost-sharing programs.

Critical to the success of shad restoration is passage around dams. Today, shad are blocked from historic spawning waters in 15 rivers by at least 78 dams that have no fish ladders or elevators. Yet even fish passage facilities are not enough. They must be supplemented by placing fertilized eggs and juvenile shad in specific river areas. Another technique, though more difficult, is to catch prespawning adults and release them directly into historic spawning areas. Unfortunately, stocking will not reverse the decline unless spawning habitat is improved.

During the 1970s fertilized shad roe was sent from the Columbia River back to Chesapeake Bay streams. The U.S. Fish and Wildlife Service in their bulletin did not say whether this has helped the runs.

Where to Fish for Shad State by State

WEST COAST

Washington State

Just below Bonneville Dam, starting at the boat deadline, downstream about three miles you'll find good fishing from both bank and boat. As previously discussed, with a fish-finder good fishing can be had from the mouth on up to Bonneville Dam.

There are other popular areas in the river where fishermen congregate in their boats. Across from the town of Camas, about 40 miles downstream, is a wide bar where numerous boats anchor during the run. Close to this is the mouth of the Washougal, which flows through the town of Washougal. Fishing can sometimes be good in this area.

Downriver from the Washougal there are three more rivers rumored to have good shad fishing. Then, not far from the mouth of the Columbia is the Elochoman River that at times has good fishing. There is no information concerning shad runs in the rivers along the Washington coast.

Oregon

Oregon shares the Columbia River with Washington. Starting at Bonneville Dam, there is both boat and bank fishing extending downriver. About 40 miles downstream from Bonneville Dam is the mouth of the Sandy River, which at times has shad fishing. Below the mouth of the Sandy River, about 15 miles, is a major tributary, the Willamette River, with an excellent run. The popular place to fish this river is at Willamette Falls where numerous boats anchor in what is popularly called a "hog line." This is something I stay away from. I am sure there are numerous other locations in the Willamette River where a fish-finder can find good shad fishing.

The coast of Oregon has numerous rivers, some have small shad runs and are seldom fished. The Siuslaw River has a good run, and the Umpqua River, about 260 miles from the California border, has an excellent shad run. This river is famous for offering wading and fly fishing for shad.

California

Shad fishing is very popular in California. The best river is the Yuba, from its mouth upstream to Dagurre Point Dam. Also popular for shad fishing is the Feather River from its mouth to the fish barrier at Oroville, the American River from its mouth to Nimbus Dam and the Sacramento River, especially in the vicinity of the mouth of Butte Creek. At times, the Department of Fish and Game claims the San Joaquin, Russian, Klamath and Trinity Rivers have good shad runs.

The time to fish in California is about the same as in Oregon, mid-May to about July 1.

EAST COAST

Shad are found in the rivers from Maine to Florida. The northern states from Virginia to Maine are fished from an anchored boat or from the bank. The southern states have long, slow meandering rivers with only rare bank fishing. The currents are so slow that trolling with small spinners or spoons is the most frequent method of fishing.

Maine

The rivers of Maine have been particularly abused by power dams, logging and pollution. The state is busy trying to restore runs of Atlantic salmon and shad. Unfortunately they have only had mediocre success with Atlantic salmon, but good success with shad. The runs are from early May to mid-June. The main shad rivers and streams frequently can be fished from the bank or waded.

The Kennebeck River is the most famous and most maligned of all of Maine's rivers. The most important improvement in the river has been decreased pollution. As yet, to my knowledge, no fish ladders have been built around Augusta Dam. Shad fishing is done in the tidal portion of this river below Augusta Dam. Boat fishing is the major method.

River	Best Location
Dennys	Dennysville
East Machias	East Machias
Pleasant	Columbia Falls
Naraguagus	Cheprifield
Kennebeck	Augusta and below
Cathanee	Bowdoinham
Eastern	Dresden
Shepscot	Alna, Newcastle
Abagadassei	Bowdoinham
Nonesuch	Scarsborough
Kennebunck	Kennebunck

Massachusetts

For reasons unknown the shad runs in some Massachusetts rivers start in mid-April and go to early June. Many of these rivers suffered from the same fate as Maine rivers. The state of Massachusetts has a successful, vigorous program of restoring shad runs in its rivers, especially the Connecticut River, where they have reduced pollution. They have put in a fish ladder at Holyoke, below which there is excellent fishing. There are new ladders on the river at various places. The Connecticut River will soon rival the Columbia with its shad runs. The Merrimack River has also had improvements made, and it, too, has a good shad run.

Massachusetts is also blessed with small, often shallow rivers that are excellent to wade and fish. North River, with its tributary Indian Head River, is near Pembroke. The North River flows into the Atlantic Ocean at Marshfield. Palmer River near Reahoboth also flows into the ocean.

New York

New York anglers think so highly of shad fishing in the Hudson that shad are known as the "queen of the Hudson." Shad appear in the lower river in late March or early April. The best time to fish is during the slow current, just before the change in direction of the tidal flow. It is especially good during the three-quarters of an hour of dead slack tide, and tapers off as the current speeds up. Hence, the best method of fishing is trolling. The mouth of Catskill Creek and the Roellift Jensen are hot spots, but good catches are possible between Poughkeepsie and Coxsackie. In the Hudson, they seem to prefer the main channel and other deep water. This is in contradistinction to most rivers where shad are usually found 10 to 20 feet deep.

Boat launching sites: New York State owns and maintains several boat launching sites in the stretch of river between Poughkeepsie and Coxsackie.

Germantown, Columbia County, off Route 96, to North Boulevard, to the end of Anchorage Road: Hard surface launching ramp; parking for 20 cars and trailers.

Coxsackie, Green County, in the village of Coxsackie: Hard surface launching ramp; parking for 36 cars and trailers.

Athens, Green County, on Route 385 in the village of Athens: Hard surface launching ramp; parking for 25 cars.

City of Hudson, Columbia County, at the foot of Water Street: Hard surface launching ramp; parking for 46 cars and trailers.

Margaret Lewis Norie State Park, Duchess County; park is located in the village of Staatsburg, nine miles north of Poughkeepsie. Ramp operated by concession; parking for 40 cars.

There are also private ramps available for use in this area. Please consult your local sporting goods shops and marinas.

The Hudson has levels of PCB. The amount found in shad is well below FDA action level and is even lower in the roe. New York State Department of Health recommends no more than half a pound per week. However, it is wise to check with Public Health before eating Hudson River shad the next time you fish the Hudson.

New Jersey

Delaware River's best area is upstream from Trenton. The run starts in mid-April and lasts until the last week in May. The Delaware has poor fishing when the water is muddy. At times most of the season may be ruined because of this condition. Licenses valid in New Jersey are also valid in the Delaware River on the Pennsylvania side. All river shoreline in Sussex County, part of the Delaware watershed, is open to the public. There is boat, bank and wade fishing.

Georgia

The Ogechee and Savannah Rivers are the most notable rivers for catching shad, both American shad and hickory shad. In recent years the catch rate on the Ogechee River has been about two fish per eight hours fishing, per angler. The middle to upper reaches, where there is clear water, is best. In the Savannah River the best fishing is below the new Savannah Bluff Lock and Dam. There is both bank and boat fishing. The run is at its best in mid-February.

Pennsylvania

Besides the Delaware River, as described in the section on New Jersey, Pennsylvania has two other shad streams, the Schuylkill and Susquehanna rivers.

By 1970 shad in the Susquehanna River had almost become extinct. In 1976 the Susquehanna River Anadromous Fish Restoration Committee was founded to supervise and fund restoration. Under their guidance hatchery production of fingerling shad and passage facilities over four power dams were accomplished. Every year since then the shad run has rapidly become larger.

Unfortunately, the Pennsylvania Fish and Boat Commission does not publish at this time a list of locations for bank and boat shad fishing. They do have a telephone number, the "Shad Hot Line", which tells the angler time, size and location of the run (610-954-0577 or 0578).

North Carolina

The two most important areas of recreational fishing for American shad are the Cape Fear and Neuse rivers. The Cape Fear River shad fishery has developed since 1962. In that year a cooperative agreement between the North Carolina Wildlife Commission, U.S. Fish and Wildlife Service and the Corps of Engineers allowed passage through the three locks on the river and restored many miles to spawning fish. Primary recreational fishing areas for hickory shad are the Neuse, Tar and Chown rivers. A favorite area for angling and drift gill nets on the Neuse River is at Springgarden and Pitch Kettle Creek, above New Bern. The shad fishery is a locally-important social event and during the spawning run fish are sold and cooked on the river bank.

Popular Shad Areas with Public Access

River	Location
Neuse	Springgarden
Neuse	Cow Pen Landing
Neuse	Pitch Kettle Creek
Pitch Kettle Creek	Craven Co.
Conrandle Creek	Grifton
Neuse	Kingston
Neuse	Goldsborough
Tar Grimsland	
Tar Tarborough	
Tar Rocky Mountain	
Cape Fear	Lock and Dams #1, 2, 3

South Carolina and Georgia

All of South Carolina's major coastal rivers support shad populations. The Edisto, Cumbahee and Ashepoo at one time had large shad runs. Mr. John W. McCord, Fin Fish Management Director, does not feel at present time they have sufficient numbers of shad to supply good fishing. All the other coastal rivers have satisfactory shad runs. Best shad streams are: the Waccmaw, Dede, Santee and Savannah. The Dede is located below Blewett Falls Dam near Rockingham. The dam is a migration barrier for anadromous fish, including shad, from this point up. The Santee River supports the largest shad run in South Carolina and is thought by some to be the largest in the Southeast. The best places to fish this river are in the Rediversion Canal below the St. Stephen's Dam, several miles below Wilson Dam on the old Santee River channel. The Cooper River's best fishing is below Pinopls's Dam.

The Savannah River has excellent fishing below Augusta lock and dam, near Augusta, Georgia, and near the mouth of several clearwater streams entering the river channel. Two such clearwater streams on the South Carolina side of the river are Steel Creek in Barnwell County and Three Runs Creek in Allendale County. Fishing the creek mouths from an anchored boat with jigs, darts and spoons is excellent. Fishing below Augusta Dam is usually from the bank, starting from the dam skirt or riprap on the Georgia side, and from a boat anchored near the riprap, or from the riprap down the South Carolina side. Access on the South Carolina side is generally by boat, on the Georgia side by auto or boat. Hickory shad are also caught in the above-mentioned rivers and are considered an incidental fish. Hickory shad stocks are much more diminished in the southern states than American Shad.

Virginia
Following are Virginia's best shad spots:
    Eastern shore at Chincoteague
    Pamunkey, Mattaponi rivers
    Aylett to West Point (Matt), Route 360 to West Point (Pam)
    Chickahominy River
    Lanexa—Walkers Dam
    Rappahannock River
    Below Fredricksburg
    Nottoway River
    Cortland to Riverdale
    Meherrin River at Emporia

Shad populations in Virginia are down. Catch and release only. Also check with Saltwater Fishing Association, Claude Bain, Suite 102, Hauser Bldg., 986 Oriole Drive S., Virginia Beach, VA 23451, (804) 491-5160.

Florida
The most popular shad river in Florida is the St. Johns River. Very few other rivers are mentioned as having shad runs.

How to
Bone a Shad

Source: Washington State Department of Fisheries

*S*ome anglers are intimidated by the prospect of cleaning shad which is a bony fish. Although you may not do it well the first time, do not be discouraged if the fish looks a bit ragged when you are done. It will taste just as good.

Also bear in mind that there are ways of enjoying shad on your dinner table that do not require traditional filleting first.

These photos and descriptions are not a complete guide to filleting, but should help you get started.

1. Place the fish on a board. Have a good, sharp filet knife and hold the shad firmly.

2. Cut off the head and tail, taking the innards out and cutting out the fins, bone and all. If you are going to cook the whole fish it is not necessary to scale it. The shad is now ready for baking. For other cooking methods scale the fish. Shad have sharp scales on the belly so take care that you do not cut yourself.

3. For filleting, the next step is to cut off the lower belly wall (the piece shown at the bottom of the photo).

4. Split the shad open and take out the backbone.

5. If boneless shad strips are desired, cut away the ribs.

6. Feel for the rows of bones in the flesh and carefully cut the meat away from the bones and skin. Shown at far right in the photo is your final shad filet strip.

Favorite Recipes

Cooking Shad

Once a shad is de-boned, it is one of the most delicious fish there is to eat. The simplest form of cooking is the best. Cooking with a lot of herbs, spices, wine, etc., destroys its marvelous flavor. The same is true of shad roe.

Broiled Shad

Place the shad fillet in a tin or glass broiling pan, skin side down. Dot with small pieces of butter, squeeze on lemon juice, sprinkle with salt and pepper, and add a dash of paprika. Broil approximately 5 to 10 minutes depending on size and thickness of fillet.

Smoked Shad

The fillets should be brined. An easy brine is composed of these proportions:

1/2 cup white sugar
1/2 cup salt (some say to use the noniodized variety)
1/2 teaspoon dill (to every cup of the above mixture)

Place fillet in non-aluminum container (aluminum is slightly soluble in brine), skin side down. Spread the brine mixture thickly over the fillet and refrigerate for four hours. Longer than this makes the fish too salty.

I use an electric smoker. The smoker has a small burner in the bottom.

Alder or hickory chips are placed in a container similar to a small frying pan. Above the stove are a series of racks that usually can be removed from the top of the aluminum box. The fillets are placed on these racks, while the wood chips are smoldering and smoking from the stove underneath.

Shad fillets are usually about 1/2 an inch to 1 and 1/2 inches thick so it is very easy to oversmoke giving you very hard and dry fillets. Hence, examine them about every 1/2 hour. They should still be moist when they are cooked.

Shad fillets should be kept in the refrigerator no longer than one week. If wrapped in plastic wrap and frozen, they will be good when thawed, even a year or two later.

Shad Roe

Wash shad roe carefully; don't break the membrane. If you do, you may have eggs all over your kitchen.

Sauté in butter on medium heat for 5 to 10 minutes, depending on size, turn once.

To the butter in the pan, add lemon juice, salt and pepper. Use as a sauce and spread over the cooked roe.

Canning Shad

Shad can well. When canned, all the bone dissolves and the end result does not taste like shad but more like canned tuna.

Improper canning can cause deadly botulism. As a physician, I can assure you that mortality from botulism is still severe. I have successfully canned shad but before you do I suggest sending for "Canning Seafood". Price: 25 cents. Oregon State University Extension Service, Corvallis, OR 97333-9800.

Bon appetite!